West Chicago Public Library District
118 West Washington
West Chicago, IL 60185-2803
Phone # (630) 231-1552

Amazing Animals
Bald Eagles

Arlene Worsley

WEIGL PUBLISHERS INC.

Published by Weigl Publishers Inc.
350 5th Avenue, Suite 3304
New York, NY USA 10118-0069

Amazing Animals series copyright © 2007
WEIGL PUBLISHERS INC. www.weigl.com

Library of Congress Cataloging-in-Publication
Data

Worsley, Arlene.
  Bald eagles / Arlene Worsley.
    p. cm. – (Amazing animals series)
  ISBN 1-59036-388-4 (hard cover : alk. paper)
– ISBN 1-59036-394-9 (soft cover : alk. paper)
  1. Bald eagle–Juvenile literature. I. Title. II.
Series.
  QL696.F32W677 2006
  598.9'43–dc22

2005027262

Printed in the United States of America
2 3 4 5 6 7 8 9 0 12 11 10 09 08

COVER: The bald eagle is a symbol of
strength in the United States. It plays an
important role in American art, folklore,
and music.

Editor
Heather C. Hudak
Design and Layout
Terry Paulhus

About This Book

This book tells you all about bald
eagles. Find out where they live
and what they eat. Discover how
you can help to protect them. You
can also read about them in myths
and legends from around
the world.

Words in **bold** are explained in the
Words to Know section at the back
of the book.

Useful Websites

Addresses in this book
take you to the home pages of
websites that have information
about bald eagles.

All of the Internet URLs given in the
book were valid at the time of
publication. However, due to the
dynamic nature of the Internet, some
addresses may have changed, or sites
may have ceased to exist since
publication. While the author and
publisher regret any inconvenience this
may cause readers, no responsibility
for any such changes can be accepted
by either the author or the publisher.

Contents

Meet the Bald Eagle

Bald eagles are powerful birds. They have long, broad wings that help them fly. Bald eagles are **raptors**. Like other raptors, bald eagles hunt for their food.

Bald eagles are not bald. They have white feathers on their head, neck, and tail. Dark brown feathers cover their body. Bald eagles have razor-sharp **talons**. These talons are their most important weapon.

▶ From tip to tip, bald eagle wings can stretch to 7 feet (2 meters).

The Eagle Family

There are many different types of eagles.

- golden eagles
- harpy eagles
- Philippine eagles
- snake eagles
- Spanish imperial eagles
- wedge-tailed eagles

▲ Bald eagles stay with the same mate for life.

How Bald Eagles Fly

The bald eagle's body is made for soaring high in the sky. Its skeleton weighs half a pound (0.23 kilograms). Its bones are light because they are **hollow**. Tough protein material called keratin makes up the beak, talons, and feathers.

The bald eagle's long wings are powerful. Strong winds help bald eagles soar. By riding these winds, bald eagles can fly for a long time without flapping their wings.

▼ Groups of eagles gather together around a plentiful food source.

Long, broad wings are used for soaring.

Bald eagles have brown feathers on their body.

Bald eagles have white feathers on their head and neck.

Keen eyesight helps bald eagles spot prey.

Sharp, yellow beaks help bald eagles tear apart **prey**.

Sharp talons are used to catch prey.

Bald eagles have white feathers on their tail.

A Very Special Animal

The big, yellow feet of bald eagles are very special. A bald eagle's feet are large in comparison to its body size. Bald eagles have rough bumps on the underside of their feet called spicules. These bumps help bald eagles hold on to slippery prey, such as fish.

▼ To catch fish, a bald eagle quickly drops down to the surface of the water with its feet stretched open.

Bald eagles have four toes, three in front and one at the back. The hind toe and talon are very powerful. The back talon is about 3 inches (8 centimeters) long.

The Amazing Bald Eagle

- Bald eagles can dive from the air at 100 miles (160 kilometers) per hour.

- Bald eagles can fly 10,000 feet (3,048 meters) above land.

- Bald eagles can swim. They swim to catch fish and carry them to shore.

▲ Bald eagles use their wings to help them move through water as they hunt for fish.

How Bald Eagles Hunt

Bald eagles are skilled hunters. They can spot fish from high above water. When an eagle spots its prey, it quickly swoops down with its talons stretched open. This action is called stooping.

Bald eagles stoop to catch fish, snakes, and small animals. They use their hooked beaks to tear their food. Like other birds, bald eagles have no teeth. Food is swallowed in pieces.

▶ About 90 percent of a bald eagle's diet is fish.

What a Meal!

- Bald eagles have a pouch, called a crop, in which to store food. The crop is located halfway between the mouth and the stomach. A full-grown bald eagle can store about 33 ounces (925 grams) of food in its crop.

- Bald eagles eat other birds, such as swans, geese, and ducks.

- Bald eagles eat about 6 to 11 percent of their body weight per day.

▼ Bald eagles often steal food from other birds and animals.

Where Do They Live?

Bald eagles live only in North America. They often live near water. Eagles build their nests, or aeries, where there is plenty of food to eat and open space to hunt.

A good **perching** area is also very important. Eagles rest and watch for prey while perching on tall trees, cliffs, or poles.

▼ Bald eagles build their nests on large trees or rocks.

Bald Eagle Range

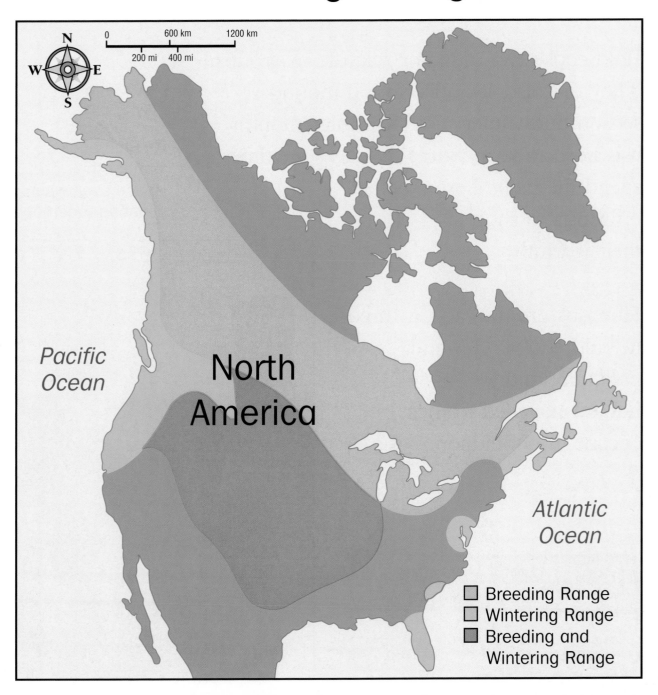

Pacific
Ocean

North
America

Atlantic
Ocean

0   600 km   1200 km
200 mi   400 mi

N
W   E
S

☐ Breeding Range
☐ Wintering Range
☐ Breeding and
   Wintering Range

Friends and Enemies

Bald eagles live alone or **migrate** in groups. They are also sociable during mating season and winter. During winter months, it is hard to keep warm. Eagles sometimes spend the night close together on **roosts** to share their warmth.

Humans are the biggest threat to bald eagles. Hunting, pollution, and loss of **habitat** have led to their decline in population.

▼ Bald eagles protect their own space even when roosting together.

Useful Websites
www.baldeagleinfo.com

Learn how bald eagles migrate by clicking on Eagle Migration on this website.

▲ Strong winds help bald eagles soar in the sky for hours at a time.

Eagle Talk

Bald eagles communicate with other animals in different ways.

- Bald eagles make high-pitch calling sounds to greet a mate or warn off an intruder.

- An eagle will chase or circle over an intruder when defending its **territory**.

Growing Up

A newly hatched baby eagle, called an eaglet, weighs as much as a tennis ball. Eaglets are born with fluffy light-gray feathers called down. The parents keep them warm by sitting next to them in the aerie. Keeping eaglets warm is called brooding.

Eagle parents are **attentive** to their young. They are quick to bring food when eaglets are hungry. Eagle parents are also protective and guard their nest at all times.

▶ The largest eaglet usually fights for the most food from its parents.

Growth Chart

Birth	3.2 ounces (91 g)	Eaglets are born with light-gray feathers, pink legs, and a wobbly neck.
4 weeks	5 pounds (2.3 kg)	Eaglets have started growing adult feathers and have learned to stand.
8 to 14 weeks	11 pounds (5 kg)	Young eagles, called juveniles, learn to fly and wander from the nest.
4 to 5 years old	10 to 14 pounds (4.5 to 6.3 kg)	Bald eagles have their adult feathers. At this time, they are able to mate.

▲ At about 4 months old, eaglets appear larger than their parents because of their longer feathers.

Under Threat

Bald eagles were once very common in North America. Their population started to decline in the 1800s. Humans began hunting bald eagles for sport. By 1921, bald eagles were facing **extinction**.

In the 1940s, people organized rescue efforts to save bald eagles. It is now against the law to hunt bald eagles in the United States.

Other human–made threats to the bald eagle include power lines, pesticides, and pollution.

▼ Bald eagles will search through garbage to find food.

Useful Websites

http://baldeagles.org/

Visit this website to learn how to help protect the bald eagle.

What Do You Think?

Pesticides help farmers grow food, such as fruits and vegetables. They are used to help control weeds or insects on food. Pesticides are also poisonous and can harm birds and animals. Should farmers be allowed to use pesticides to help them grow food? Should farmers create another chemical that is friendly to the environment?

▲ Bald eagle populations declined as the use of pesticides became more widespread.

Myths and Legends

Romans and Greeks believed that eagles had healing powers. In ancient Babylon, the souls of rulers were believed to rise to heaven on an eagle.

Bald eagles also represented strength, pride, and power. Warriors admired these majestic birds. Bald eagles are also national emblems in many countries. The bald eagle has been the national bird of the United States since 1782.

Many people have told interesting stories about the bald eagle.

▶ In an engraving by Edward Savage, the goddess of youth supports a bald eagle.

Aztec Myth

Ancient Aztecs believed that, during the creation of the present world, the eagle and the jaguar fought over who would have the honor of becoming the Sun. The eagle flung himself into a fire and became the Sun. The jaguar followed behind and became the Moon.

▶ This statue of the Aztec Eagle Warrior dates back to around AD 1440 to 1469.

Quiz

1. What are the bald eagle's sharp claws called?

(a) nails (b) hooks (c) talons

2. What are baby bald eagles called?

(a) piglets (b) eaglets (c) chicks

3. What is another name for a bald eagle's nest?

(a) aerie (b) perch (c) roost

4. What color are an eaglet's feathers at birth?

(a) light-gray (b) brown (c) white

5. What is the name of an eaglet's feathers?

(a) cotton (b) down (c) plumage

Answers:
1. (c) A bald eagle's sharp claws are called talons.
2. (b) Baby bald eagles are called eaglets.
3. (a) Another name for a bald eagle's nest is aerie.
4. (a) An eaglet's feathers are light-gray at birth.
5. (b) An eaglet's feathers are called down.

Find out More

To find out more about bald eagles, visit the websites in this book. You can also write to these organizations.

**American Bald
Eagle Foundation**
P.O. Box 49
113 Haines Highway
Haines, AK 99827

National Wildlife Federation
11100 Wildlife Center Drive
Reston, VA 20190-5362

**Alaska Chilkat Bald
Eagle Preserve**
400 Willoughby, 4th Floor
Juneau, AK 99801

Words to Know

attentive
paying careful attention to

extinction
at risk of no longer living on Earth

habitat
the natural environment in which animals
and plants live

hollow
having an empty space inside

migrate
to move from place to place depending
on the season

perching
sitting and watching

prey
animals that are hunted by other
animals for food

raptors
birds of prey

roosts
trees where eagles rest

talons
a bird's razor-sharp claws

territory
an area that animals protect from intruders

Index